The Joy of Rare Piano Pieces

Compiled and edited by Denes Agay.

Yorktown Music Press / Music Sales Limited

London / New York / Paris / Sydney / Copenhagen / Madrid

Order No. YK 21718
US International Standard Book Number: 0.8256.8092.1
UK International Standard Book Number: 0.7119.5413.5

Exclusive Distributors:
Music Sales Corporation
257 Park Avenue South, New York, NY 10010 USA
Music Sales Limited
8/9 Frith Street, London W1V 5TZ England
Music Sales Pty. Limited
120 Rothschild Street, Rosebery, Sydney, NSW 2018, Australia

Printed in the United States of America by
Vicks Lithograph and Printing Corporation

Contenrs

Forlana*

Gottlieb Muffat
(1690–1770)

* Old Italian folk dance, favorite of the Venetian gondoliers

Old French Dance

Anonymous
(18th Century)

Minuetto Scherzando

Francesco Pasquale Ricci
(1732–1817)

Allegretto

Aria Pastorella

Johann Valentin Rathgeber
(1682–1750)

Andantino

Fine

D.C. al Fine

Gavotte

Georg Philipp Telemann
(1681–1767)

Andantino con grazia

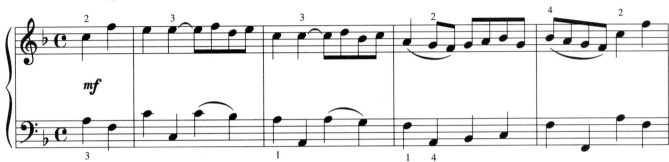

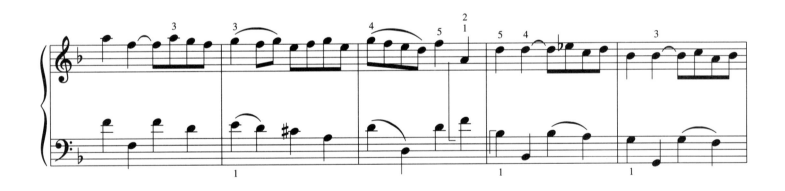

Fine

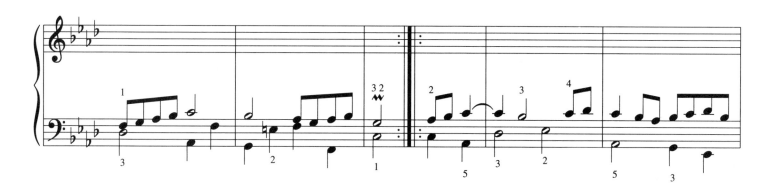

D.C. al Fine

Canzone*

George Frideric Handel
(1685–1759)

Moderato

* From an 18th century manuscript collection.

Echo Minuet

Johann Nikolaus Tischer
(1707–1774)

English Dance

Karl Ditters von Dittersdorf
(1739–1799)

Allegro

Divertimento

Josef Mysliveček
(1737–1781)

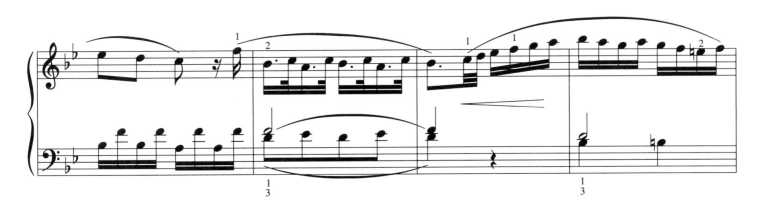

Romance

William Crotch
(1775–1847)

Sonatina
No. 19

Jiři Antonin Benda
(1722–1795)

Allegretto

Rondo Espressivo

from Sonata No. 3 (1779)

Carl Philipp Emanuel Bach
(1714–1788)

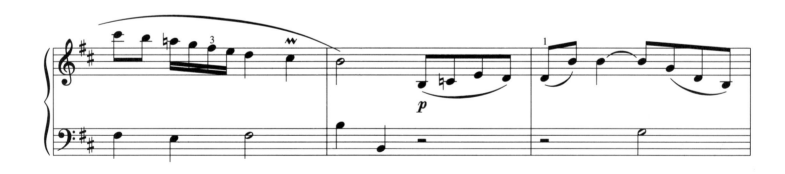

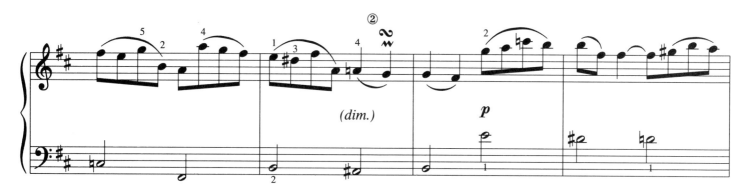

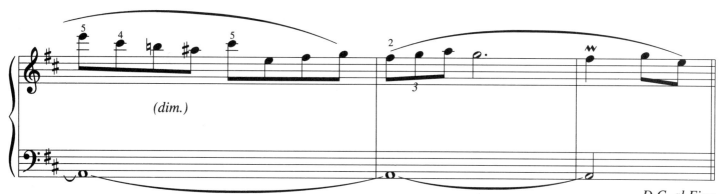

D.C. al Fine

The Viennese Clock*
1. Andantino

Franz Joseph Haydn
(1732–1809)

* Haydn composed these pieces for a tiny "flute organ" operated by a clock mechanism.

Segue

2. Song of the Quail

"Andantino" may be repeated

Minuetto Dramatico

Friedrich L. Kunzen*
(1761–1817)

Con moto

* *Born in Germany, active in Denmark*

Mazurka

Maria Agata Szymanowska
(1789–1831)

Allegretto

Rondo Finale
(from a Sonatina in E)

Ernst Wilhelm Wolf
(1735–1792)

Allegro

Variations On a French Song

Wilhelm Friedemann Bach
(1710–1784)

Allegretto

* Dynamic marks in parenthesis refer to repetitions

Variation 1

From a collection of diverse pieces printed in 1804. The authorship of W.F. Bach is somewhat questionable. The diatonic simplicity and lighthearted rococo charm of the work are more characteristic of the gallant style of his two younger brothers, Johann Christoph Friedrich or Johann Christian Bach.

Variation 2

Variation 3

Variation 4

Schwäbisch

Variation 5

alla Siciliana

Variation 6   **Poco più lento**

Variation 7   **Allegro**

Rondo Scherzando

from Sonatina in B♭ (1792)

Johann Georg Witthauer
(1751–1802)

Allegro giocoso

Polonaise

Michal Kleofas Ogiński
(1765–1833)

Moderato, molto cantabile

Trio

First Love

Old Hungarian Serenade

Edited by Denes Agay

Jozsef Kossovits
(1750–1819)

* *This famous melody was until recently attributed to János Lavotta (1764–1820)*

Tempo I

Song

from Op. 33

Adolf Jensen
(1837–1879)

Rondeau Bohemienne

Franz Lauska
(1764–1825)

Allegretto

Spanish Dance

Édouard Lalo
(1823–1892)

Allegro moderato

sempre staccato

Little Prelude

from "L'Organiste"

César Franck
(1822–1890)

Quasi andante

Reminiscence

from Op. 57

Zdeněk Fibich
(1850–1900)

Tenderly moving

Song of Youth

Op. 45, No. 1

Agathe Backer–Grøndahl
(1847–1907)

Tranquillo (♩. = 52)

Prelude

Op. 31, No. 23

Charles-Valentin Alkan
(1813–1888)

Serenade

from Petite Suite

Alexander Borodin
(1833–1887)

Allegretto

Valse

Peter Ilyich Tchaikovsky
(1840–1893)

Moderato

Album Leaf

André Messager
(1853–1929)

Allegretto

This originally untitled composition was written by Messager as a test piece for the examination of sight-reading ability at the Conservatoire of Paris.

Polka Italienne

Sergei Rachmaninoff
(1873–1943)

Originally written as a piano duet. The solo version most likely is either by the composer or by Alexander Siloti to whom the work is dedicated.

(D.C al Fine)

The Teddy Bear

from "Les Amusements de Ferkó," Op.41, No.3

Albert Siklós
(1878–1942)

Allegretto giocoso

Childhood Memories

from "Stories for the Young"

Enrique Granados
(1867–1916)

Village Dance

Vitězslav Novák
(1870–1949)

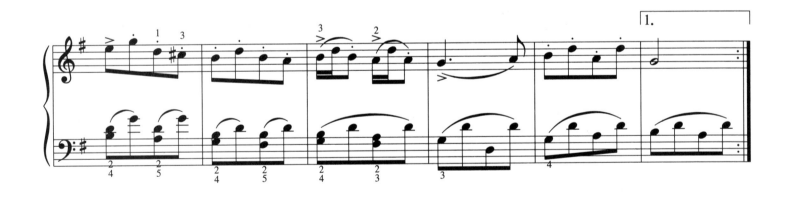

A Blown Away Leaf

from "The Overgrown Path"

Leoš Janáček
(1854–1928)

Prelude
Op. 31, No. 1

Reinhold Glière
(1875–1956)

Andante (♩ = 60)

Valse
Op. 2

Mischa Levitzki
(1898–1941)

A Ballad Told at Candlelight

Cyril Scott
(1879–1970)

Tempo di marcia

A Quiet Song

Nikolay Petrovich Rakov
(1908–)

Three Polish Folk Melodies
1. Flirting

Witold Lutoslawski
(1913–1994)

2. The Gander

Andantino (♩ = ca. 92)

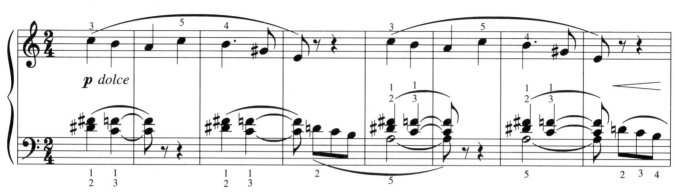

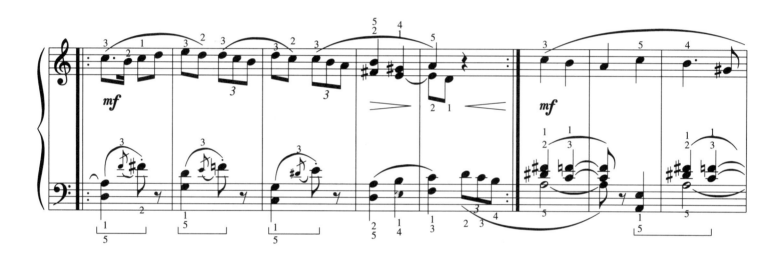

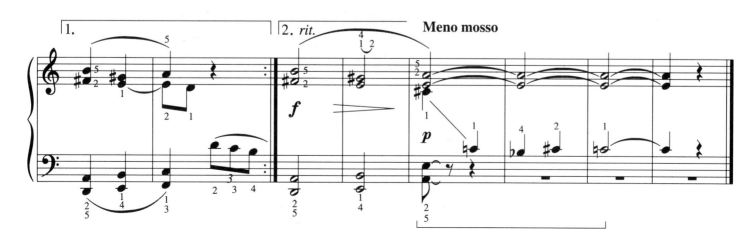

3. The Grove

Allegro vivace (♩ = ca. 88)

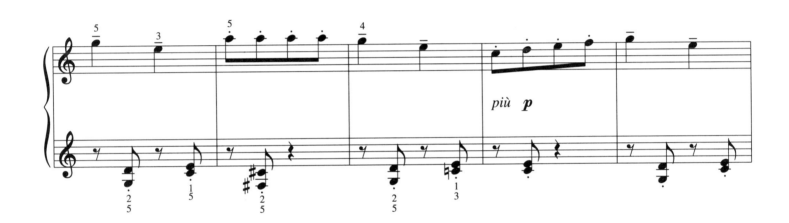

Lyric Interlude

Op. 53, No. 13

Carl Nielsen
(1865–1931)

Moment Musical

Op. 80, No.1

Eduard Poldini
(1886–1957)

Cradle Song

Alexander Dubyansky
(1900–1920)